100

things you should know about

REPTILES &
AMPHIBIANS

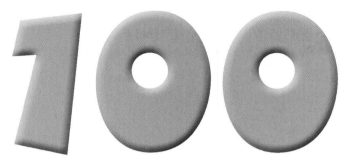

100

things you should know about

REPTILES &
AMPHIBIANS

Ann Kay
Consultant: Steve Parker

Miles Kelly
PUBLISHING

First published in 2005 by
Miles Kelly Publishing Ltd
Bardfield Centre, Great Bardfield, Essex, CM7 4SL

Copyright © Miles Kelly Publishing Ltd 2005

This edition printed in 2008

2 4 6 8 10 9 7 5 3

Editorial Director: Belinda Gallagher
Art Director: Jo Brewer
Project Editor, Copy Editor: Neil de Cort
Editorial Assistant: Nicola Sail
Designer: Angela Ashton
Picture Research: Liberty Newton
Proof Reading, Indexing: Jane Parker

ISBN 978-1-84236-355-3

Printed in China

ACKNOWLEDGEMENTS
The Publishers would like to thank the following artists who have
contributed to this book:

Susanna Addario/ Scientific Illustration
Andy Beckett/ Illustration Limited
Peter Bull Art Studio
Jim Channell/ Bernard Thornton Artists
Richard Draper
Mike Foster/ Maltings Partnership
Wayne Ford
Chris Forsey
L.R. Galante/ Studio Galante
Alan Hancocks
Kevin Maddison

Alan Male/ Linden Artists
Janos Marffy
Doreen McGuiness/ Illustration Limited
Terry Riley
Martin Sanders
Mike Saunders
Rob Sheffield
Rudi Vizi
Christian Webb/ Temple Rogers
Steve Weston/ Linden Artists

Cartoons by Mark Davis at Mackerel

www.mileskelly.net
info@mileskelly.net

www.factsforprojects.com

Contents

Cold-blooded creatures

1 **Reptiles and amphibians are cold-blooded animals.** This means that they cannot control their body temperature like we can. A reptile's skin is dry and scaly, most reptiles spend much of their time on land. Most amphibians live in or around water. The skin of an amphibian is smooth and wet.

Nile crocodiles

Golden arrow-poison frog

Common frog

Spotted salamander

Eastern green
mamba snake

Komodo dragon

Indian cobra

Desert
tortoise

Jackson's
chameleon

Shingleback
lizard

Frilled lizard

Scales and slime

2 Reptiles and amphibians can be divided into smaller groups. There are four kinds of reptiles, snakes and lizards, the crocodile family, tortoises and turtles and the tuatara. Amphibians are split into frogs and toads, newts and salamanders, and caecilians.

▲ Crocodiles are the largest reptiles in the world. Their eyes and nostrils are placed high on their heads so that they can stay mostly under water while approaching their prey.

3 Reptiles do a lot of sunbathing! They do this, called basking, to get themselves warm with the heat from the sun so that they can move about. When it gets cold, at night or during a cold season, they might sleep, or they might hibernate, which means that they go into a very deep sleep.

4 Most reptiles have dry, scaly, waterproof skin. This stops their bodies from drying out. The scales are made of keratin and may form very thick, tough plates. Human nails are also made of the same sort of material.

▲ This reptile, an agama lizard from Africa, gets itself warm by lying, or basking, in the sun.

5 The average amphibian has skin that is moist, fairly smooth and soft. Oxygen can pass easily through their skin, which is important because most adult amphibians breathe through their skin as well as with their lungs. Reptiles breathe only through their lungs.

6 Amphibians' skin is kept moist by special glands just under the surface. These glands produce a sticky substance called mucus. Many amphibians also keep their skin moist by making sure that they are never far away from water.

QUIZ

1. Are reptiles warm– or cold–blooded?
2. Are amphibians warm or cold–blooded?
3. Can you think how these creatures might warm up?
4. How do reptiles breathe?
5. How do amphibians breathe?

1. Cold-blooded. 2. Cold-blooded. 3. By a spot of sunbathing! 4. Through their lungs. 5. Through their skin and lungs.

▶ Oxygen passes in through the skin and into the blood, while carbon dioxide passes out.

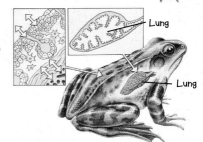

Lung

Lung

7 Some amphibians have no lungs. Humans breathe with their lungs to get oxygen from the air and breathe out carbon dioxide. Most amphibians breathe through their skin and lungs, but lungless salamanders breathe only through their skin and the lining of the mouth.

Sun worshippers

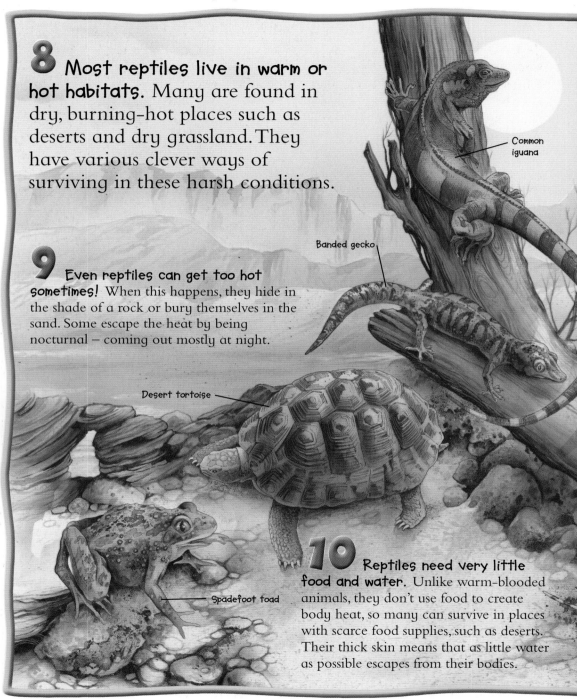

8 **Most reptiles live in warm or hot habitats.** Many are found in dry, burning-hot places such as deserts and dry grassland. They have various clever ways of surviving in these harsh conditions.

9 **Even reptiles can get too hot sometimes!** When this happens, they hide in the shade of a rock or bury themselves in the sand. Some escape the heat by being nocturnal – coming out mostly at night.

10 **Reptiles need very little food and water.** Unlike warm-blooded animals, they don't use food to create body heat, so many can survive in places with scarce food supplies, such as deserts. Their thick skin means that as little water as possible escapes from their bodies.

Common iguana

Banded gecko

Desert tortoise

Spadefoot toad

11 Reptiles need a certain level of warmth to survive. This is why there are no reptiles in very cold places, such as at the North and South Poles, or at the very tops of mountains.

Banded gecko

12 Like reptiles, many amphibians live in very hot places. But sometimes it can get too hot and dry for them. The spadefoot toad from Europe, Asia and North America buries itself in the sand to escape the heat and dryness.

Leopard lizard

Zebratail lizard

North American puff adder

11

Cooler customers

13 Many amphibians are common in cooler, damper parts of the world. Amphibians like wet places. Most mate and lay their eggs in water.

14 As spring arrives, amphibians come out of hiding. The warmer weather sees many amphibians returning to the pond or stream where they were born. This may mean a very long journey through towns or over busy roads.

I DON'T BELIEVE IT!

Look out – frog crossing the road! In some countries, signs warn drivers of a very unusual 'hazard' ahead – frogs or toads travelling along the roads to return to breeding grounds.

15 **When the weather turns especially cold, amphibians often hide away.** They simply hibernate in the mud at the bottom of ponds or under stones and logs. This means that they go to sleep in the autumn, and don't wake up until spring!

▶ This aquatic, or water–living, salamander is called a mudpuppy. It lives in freshwater lakes, rivers and streams in North America.

16 **Journeys to breeding grounds may be up to 5 kilometres long, a long way for an animal only a few centimetres in length!** This is like a man walking to a pond 90 kilometres away without a map! The animals find their way by scent, landmarks, the Earth's magnetic field and the Sun's position.

Water babies

17 Amphibians live in water and on land. Most are born and grow up in fresh water such as ponds, pools, streams and rivers. They move onto dry land when they are adults and return to water to breed.

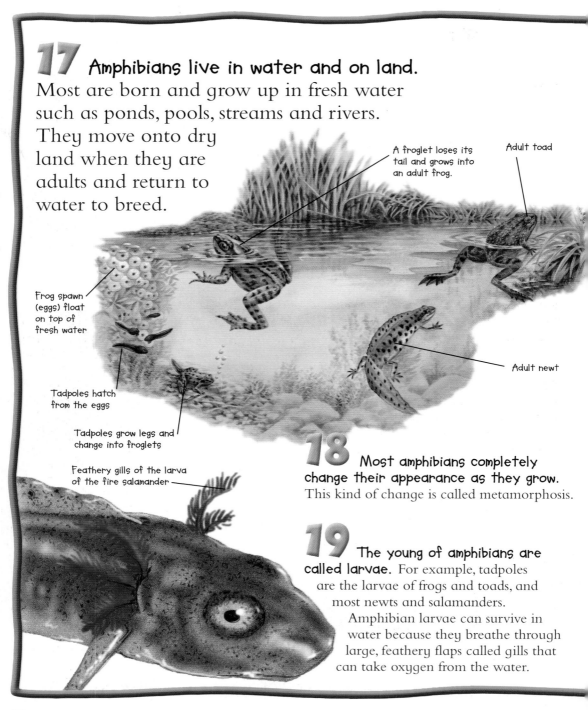

A froglet loses its tail and grows into an adult frog.

Adult toad

Frog spawn (eggs) float on top of fresh water

Tadpoles hatch from the eggs

Tadpoles grow legs and change into froglets

Feathery gills of the larva of the fire salamander

Adult newt

18 Most amphibians completely change their appearance as they grow. This kind of change is called metamorphosis.

19 The young of amphibians are called larvae. For example, tadpoles are the larvae of frogs and toads, and most newts and salamanders. Amphibian larvae can survive in water because they breathe through large, feathery flaps called gills that can take oxygen from the water.

▼ The axolotl lives only in Mexico, in the southern part of North America.

20 **The axolotl is an amphibian that has never grown up.** This type of water-living salamander has never developed beyond the larval stage. It does, however, develop far enough to be able to breed.

21 **The majority of amphibians lay soft eggs.** These may be in a jelly-like string or clump of tiny eggs called spawn, as with frogs and toads. Newts lay their eggs singly.

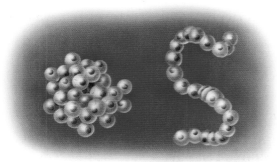

▲ Most amphibians lay their eggs in clumps or strings like these.

22 **A few amphibians give birth to live young instead of laying eggs.** The eggs of the fire salamander, for example, stay inside their mother, where the young hatch out and develop. She then gives birth to young that are much like miniature adults.

Land-lubbers

23 The majority of reptiles spend their whole lives away from water. They are very well adapted for life on dry land. Some do spend time in the water, but most reptiles lay their eggs on land.

▲ This female West African dwarf crocodile is laying her eggs in a hole, dug near to the water.

24 Most reptile eggs are much tougher than those of amphibians. This is because they must survive life out of the water. Lizards and snakes lay eggs with leathery shells. Crocodile and tortoise eggs have a hard shell rather like birds' eggs.

▲ Alligators lay their eggs in a mound of plants and earth. They lay between 35 and 40 eggs.

▲ A ground python's egg is large compared to its body. A female is about 85 centimetres long, and her eggs are about 12 centimetres long.

▲ A lizard called a Javan bloodsucker lays strange eggs like this. No one knows why their eggs are this very long and thin shape.

▲ Galapagos giant tortoises lay round eggs like this one. They will hatch up to 200 days after they were laid.

25 **The eggs feed and protect the young developing inside them.** The egg yolk provides food for the developing young, called an embryo. The shell protects the embryo from the outside world, but also allows vital oxygen into the egg.

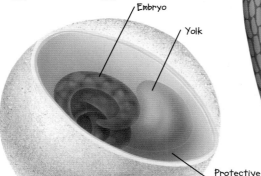

Embryo

Yolk

Protective fluid

Shell

INVESTIGATING EGGS

Reptile eggs are rather like birds' eggs. Next time you eat an omelette or boiled egg, rinse out half an empty eggshell, fill it with water, and wait a while. Do you see how no water escapes? Wash your hands well once you're done. Like this bird's eggshell, reptile eggshells stop the egg from drying out, although they let air in and are tough enough to protect the embryo.

26 **Young reptiles hatch out of eggs as miniature adults.** They do not undergo a change, or metamorphosis, like amphibians do.

◄ Slow worms are not worms at all. They are legless lizards that live in Europe, Africa and Asia. They are viviparous lizards, which means that they give birth to live young.

27 **Some snakes and lizards, like slow worms, don't lay eggs.** Instead, they give birth to fully developed live young. Animals that do this are called 'viviparous'.

Snake eggs left in the undergrowth

Little and large

28 Reptiles and amphibians come in every shape and size. There are more than 6500 species (types) of reptiles and 4000 species of amphibians. They range from tiny frogs to giant, dinosaur-like lizards.

29 The largest reptile award goes to the saltwater crocodile from around the Indian and west Pacific Oceans. It measures a staggering 8 metres from nose to tail – an average adult man is not even 2 metres tall! Cold streams in Japan are home to the largest amphibian – a giant salamander that is around 1.5 metres long, and weighs up to 40 kilograms.

▲ The saltwater or estuarine crocodile lives in southern India, Indonesia and North Australia. It is the largest and one of the most dangerous species of crocodile. The giant salamander, though, is mostly harmless and feeds on snails and worms.

QUIZ

1. Where does the world's smallest reptile come from?
2. What kind of animal is the world's largest amphibian?
3. Where does the world's largest crocodile live?
4. Which group contains more species – reptiles or amphibians?

1. The Caribbean Virgin Islands.
2. A Japanese salamander.
3. Australia and India
4. Reptiles.

30 The world's tiniest reptile is a gecko from the Caribbean Virgin Islands.
This lizard measures under 20 millimetres long. A Brazilian frog is among the smallest of amphibians. Its body length is just 9.8 millimetres, that's almost small enough to fit on your thumbnail!

◀ One type of giant tortoise comes from the Galapagos Islands in the Pacific Ocean, to the west of South America. The tortoise grows up to 1.2 metres long, and can weigh 215 kilograms.

Adaptable animals

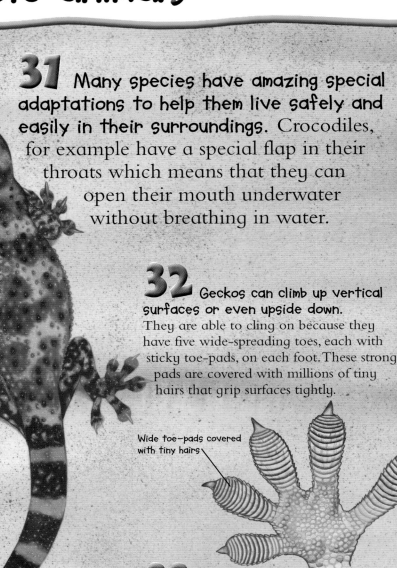

31 Many species have amazing special adaptations to help them live safely and easily in their surroundings. Crocodiles, for example have a special flap in their throats which means that they can open their mouth underwater without breathing in water.

32 Geckos can climb up vertical surfaces or even upside down. They are able to cling on because they have five wide-spreading toes, each with sticky toe-pads, on each foot. These strong pads are covered with millions of tiny hairs that grip surfaces tightly.

Wide toe-pads covered with tiny hairs

▶ This is a tokay gecko from South and Southeast Asia. It is one of the most common geckos, and also one of the largest, measuring up to 28 centimetres long. It is usually easy to find them because they like to live around houses. The people of Asia and Indonesia believe that it is good luck for a gecko to come and live by or in their house!

33 Tortoises and turtles have hard, bony shells for protection. They form a suit of armour that protects them from predators (animals who might hunt and eat them) and also from the hot sun.

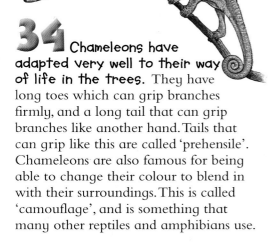

▲ California newt

34
Chameleons have adapted very well to their way of life in the trees. They have long toes which can grip branches firmly, and a long tail that can grip branches like another hand. Tails that can grip like this are called 'prehensile'. Chameleons are also famous for being able to change their colour to blend in with their surroundings. This is called 'camouflage', and is something that many other reptiles and amphibians use.

35
The flattened tails of newts make them expert swimmers. Newts are salamanders that spend most of their lives in water, so they need to be able to get about speedily in this environment.

▶ This is a very close-up view of a small part of a gill. As water flows over the gills, oxygen can pass into the amphibian's blood.

water flows over the gills

36
An amphibian's gills enable it to breathe underwater. Blood flows inside the feathery gills, at the same time as water flows over the outside. As the water flows past the gills, oxygen passes out of the water, straight into the blood of the amphibian.

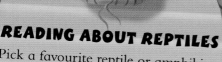

READING ABOUT REPTILES
Pick a favourite reptile or amphibian and then find out as much as you can about it. List all the ways you think it is especially well adapted to deal with its lifestyle and habitat.

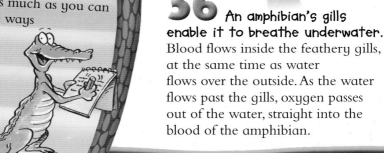

Natural show-offs

► Cobras make themselves look more threatening by forming a wide hood of loose skin stretched over flexible ribs.

37 Certain reptiles and amphibians love to make a show of themselves. Some of this 'display' behaviour is used to attract females when the breeding season comes around. It is also used to make enemies think twice before pouncing.

◄ This great crested newt from Europe is showing its colours.

38 Male newts go to great lengths to impress during the mating season. Great crested newts develop frills along their backs, black spots over their skin, and a red flush across the breast. Their colourful spring coat also warns off enemies.

39 The male anole lizard of Central and South America guards his territory and mates jealously. When rival males come too close, he puffs out a bright red throat pouch at them. Two males may face each other with inflated throats for hours at a time!

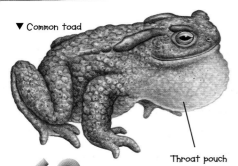

▼ Common toad

Throat pouch

40 Many frogs and toads also puff themselves up. Toads can inflate their bodies to look more frightening. Frogs and toads can puff out their throat pouches. This makes their croaking love-calls to mates, and 'back off' calls to enemies, much louder.

41 A frilled lizard in full display is an amazing sight. This lizard has a large flap of neck skin that normally lies flat. When faced by a predator, it spreads this out to form a huge, stiff ruff that makes it look bigger and scarier!

▲ The frilled lizard lives in Australia and New Guinea. Its frill can be up to 25 centimetres across, almost half the length of its body!

42 Male monitor lizards have their own wrestling competitions! At the beginning of the mating season they compete to try to win the females. They rear up on their hind legs and wrestle until the weaker animal gives up.

Sensitive creatures

43 Reptiles and amphibians find out about the world by using their senses such as sight, smell and touch. Some animals have lost senses that they don't need. Worm-like amphibians called caecilians, for example, spend their whole lives underground, so they don't have any use for eyes. However, some animals have developed new senses which are very unusual!

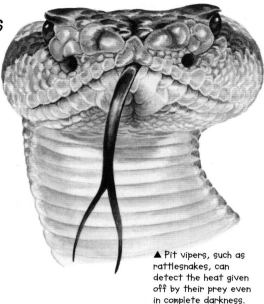

▲ Pit vipers, such as rattlesnakes, can detect the heat given off by their prey even in complete darkness.

44 Frogs and toads have developed new senses. They have something called Jacobson's organ in the roofs of their mouths. This helps them to 'taste' and 'smell' the outside world. Jacobson's organ is also found in snakes and some lizards.

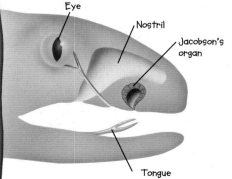

Eye

Nostril

Jacobson's organ

Tongue

45 Snakes have poor hearing and eyesight but they make up for it in other ways. They can find prey by picking up its vibrations travelling through the ground. Some snakes have pits in their faces that detect heat given off by prey. In contrast to snakes, frogs and toads have large and well-developed eardrums and very good hearing.

Ear of American bullfrog

▼ The Fijian banded iguana lives on the islands of Fiji and Tonga in the Pacific Ocean.

46 Geckos and iguanas have large eyes and very good eyesight. They are a type of lizard that can't blink. Instead of having movable eyelids like humans, they have fixed, transparent 'spectacles' over their eyes. Most lizards have very good sight – they need it to hunt down their small and fast insect prey.

Large eyes give the gecko excellent vision.

Geckos lick their eyes to keep them clean.

▲ This is a web-footed gecko from southwest Africa. It lives in the Namib Desert, where it hardly ever rains. To get the water it needs, it licks dew from the stones, and also licks its own eyes!

25

Expert hunters

47 **All amphibians and most reptiles are meat-eaters.** They use a huge variety of ways to do their tracking, trapping and hunting.

▲ Crocodiles and alligators are specially adapted to be able to lie in the water with only their eyes and nostrils showing. They wait in shallow water for animals to come and drink, then leap up and drag their prey under the water.

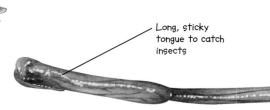

Long, sticky tongue to catch insects

48 **The chameleon lizard is a highly efficient hunting machine.** Each eye moves separately from the other, so the chameleon can look in two directions at once. When a tasty fly buzzes past, the chameleon shoots out an incredibly long tongue in a fraction of a second and draws the fly back into its mouth.

49 **Salamanders creep up slowly before striking.** They move gradually towards prey and then suddenly seize it with their tongue or between their sharp teeth.

50
Crocodiles and snakes can open their fierce jaws extra wide to eat huge dinners! A snake can separate its jaw bones to eat huge eggs or to gulp down animals much larger than its head. A large snake can swallow pigs and deer – whole!

Skull

A snake's lower jaws can work separately. First one side pulls, and then the other, to draw the prey into the throat.

The snake's lower jaws can also detach from its skull to eat large prey.

BE A CHAMELEON!

Like a chameleon, you need two eyes to judge distances easily. Here's an experiment to prove it!

Close one eye. Hold a finger out in front of you, and with one eye open, try to touch this fingertip with the other. It's not as easy as it looks! Now open both eyes and you'll find it a lot easier!

Two eyes give your brain two slightly different angles to look at the object, so it is easier to tell how far away it is!

51
A snake has to swallow things whole. This is because it has no large back teeth for crushing prey and can't chew.

The chameleon's eyes can move independently to locate a tasty insect!

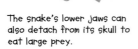

▶ Once the chameleon has spotted a tasty insect with one eye, it first has to swivel its other eye to look at the prey. This is because it is easier to judge distances with two eyes.

Fliers and leapers

52 Some reptiles and amphibians can take to the air – if only for a few seconds. This helps animals to travel further, escape predators or swoop down on passing prey before it gets away.

▶ Flying snakes can glide between branches of trees to hunt lizards and frogs.

▶ The flying dragon lizard has taken things a step further than the geckos. Its 'wings' are skin stretched out over ribs that can even fold back when they are not in use!

54 Even certain kinds of snake can glide. The flying snake lives in the tropical forests of southern Asia. It can jump between branches or glide through the air in 'S' movements.

◀ Flying geckos' skills are all important for food. Either they are trying to catch food, or they are trying to avoid becoming food for something else!

53 Gliding snakes fly by making their bodies into parachutes. They do this by raising their rib-cages so that their bodies flatten out like a ribbon.

55 Flying geckos form another group of natural parachutes. They have webbed feet and folds of skin along their legs, tail and sides, which together form the perfect gliding machine.

56 Some frogs can glide.

Deep in the steamy rainforests of southeast Asia and South America, tree frogs flit from tree to tree. Some can glide as far as 12 metres, clinging to their landing spot with suckers on their feet.

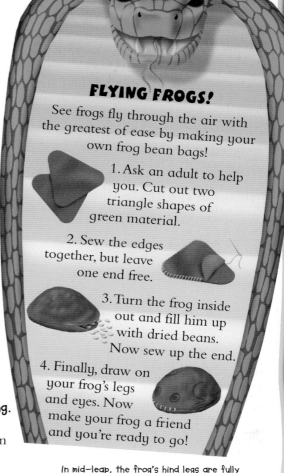

FLYING FROGS!

See frogs fly through the air with the greatest of ease by making your own frog bean bags!

1. Ask an adult to help you. Cut out two triangle shapes of green material.

2. Sew the edges together, but leave one end free.

3. Turn the frog inside out and fill him up with dried beans. Now sew up the end.

4. Finally, draw on your frog's legs and eyes. Now make your frog a friend and you're ready to go!

57 Frogs and toads use their powerful hind legs for hopping or jumping.

The greatest frog leaper comes from Africa. Known as the rocket frog, it has been known to jump up to 4.2 metres.

The powerful muscles in the frog's hind legs push off.

In mid–leap, the frog's hind legs are fully stretched out, its front legs are held back, and its eyes are closed for protection.

As it lands, its body arches and the front legs act as a brake.

Slitherers and crawlers

58 Most reptiles, and some amphibians, spend much of their time creeping, crawling and slithering along the ground. In fact, scientists call the study of reptiles and amphibians 'herpetology', which comes from a Greek word meaning 'to creep or crawl'.

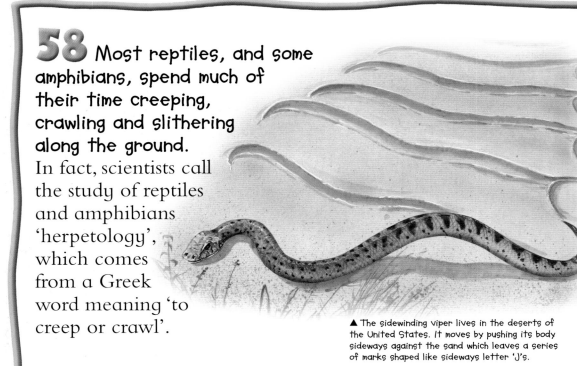

▲ The sidewinding viper lives in the deserts of the United States. It moves by pushing its body sideways against the sand which leaves a series of marks shaped like sideways letter 'J's.

59 A snake's skin does not grow with its body. This means that it has to shed its skin to grow bigger. This grass snake from Europe is slithering right out of its old skin!

60 Some frogs and toads also shed their skin. The European toad sheds its skin several times during the summer – and then eats it! This recycles the goodness in the toad's skin.

61 **Snakes and caecilians have no legs.** Caecilians are amphibians that look like worms or snakes. They move around by slithering about gracefully. Small snakes have about 180 vertebrae, or backbones. Large snakes can have 400! They have very strong muscles to enable them to move, so their backbones are also extra strong to stand up to the strain.

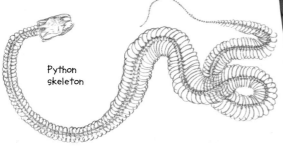

Python skeleton

SLITHER AND SLIDE!

Make your own slithery snake. First you need to collect as many cotton reels as you can, and paint them lots of bright colours. Next, cut a forked tongue and some snake eyes out of some paper and stick them onto one of the reels to make a head. Now, just thread your reels onto a piece of string. Make sure you don't put the head in the middle!

◀ This South American caecilian can reach 35 centimetres long! It feeds mostly on earthworms.

62 **A ground snake has special scales on the underside of its body.** These help it to grip the ground as it moves along.

▼ The scales on the underside of some snakes overlap. This helps it moves smoothly, and also provides the snake with more grip.

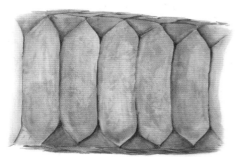

63 **Some reptiles and amphibians slither below the surface.** In hot, deserty places, snakes burrow down into the sand to escape the sun's fierce heat. Caecilians' heads are perfectly shaped to burrow through the mud of their tropical homelands, searching for worms.

Fast and slow

64 The reptile and amphibian worlds contain their fair share of fast and slow movers. But the slow-coaches are not necessarily at a disadvantage. A predator may be able to seize the slow-moving tortoise, but it certainly can't bite through its armour-plated shell!

▶ The sidewinder snake moves at up to 4 kilometres per hour over the shifting sands of its desert home.

65 Tortoises never take life in a hurry and are among the slowest animals on Earth. The top speed for a giant tortoise is 5 metres per minute! These giant tortoises live on the small Galapagos islands in the Pacific Ocean, and not anywhere else in the world.

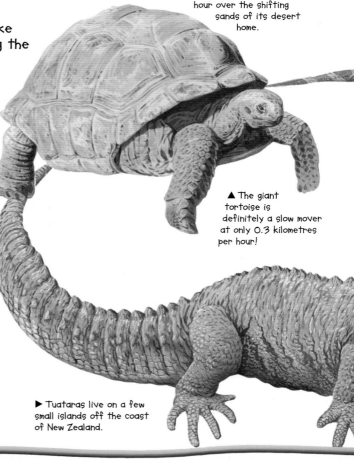

▲ The giant tortoise is definitely a slow mover at only 0.3 kilometres per hour!

66 Chameleons are also slow-movers. They move slowly through the trees, barely noticeable as they hunt for insects.

▲ The chameleon is a very slow mover, until its tongue pops out to trap a passing fly!

▶ Tuataras live on a few small islands off the coast of New Zealand.

67 Some lizards can trot off at high speed by 'standing up'. Water dragon lizards from Asia can simply rear up onto their hind legs to make a dash for it – much faster than moving on four legs.

◀ The speedy crested water dragon can run on its back legs to escape predators.

FLAT RACE

Get together a group of friends and hold your own animal race day. Each of you cuts a flat animal shape – a frog or tortoise, say – out of paper or very light card. If you wish, add details with coloured pencils or pens. Now race your animals along the ground to the finishing line by flapping a newspaper or a magazine behind them.

68 One of the world's slowest animals is the lizard–like tuatara. When resting, it breathes just once an hour, and may still be growing when it is 60 years old! Their slow lifestyle in part means that they can live to be 120 years old! The tuatara is sometimes called a 'living fossil'. This is because it is the only living species of a group of animals that died out millions of years ago. No one knows why only the tuatara survives.

69 Racerunner lizards, from North and South America, are true to their name. The six-lined racerunner is the fastest recorded reptile on land. In 1941 in South Carolina, USA it was recorded reaching an amazing speed of 29 kilometres per hour!

◀ The six-lined racerunner from America is the fastest reptile on land.

Champion swimmers

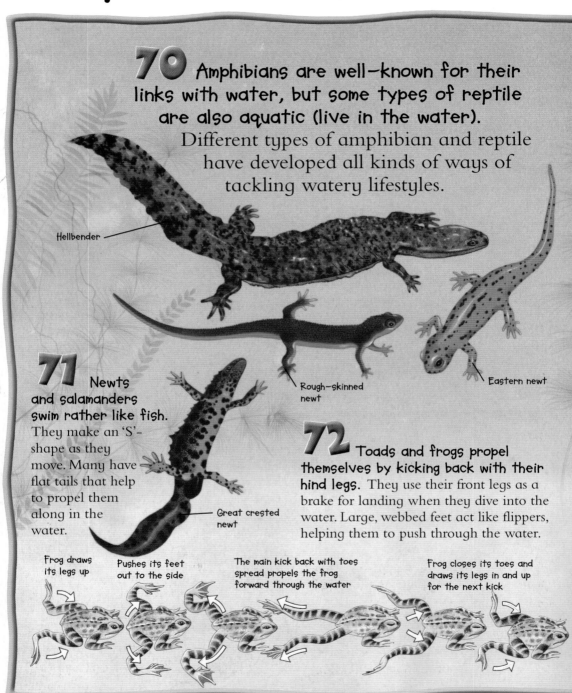

70 Amphibians are well—known for their links with water, but some types of reptile are also aquatic (live in the water). Different types of amphibian and reptile have developed all kinds of ways of tackling watery lifestyles.

Hellbender

Rough—skinned newt

Eastern newt

71 Newts and salamanders swim rather like fish. They make an 'S'-shape as they move. Many have flat tails that help to propel them along in the water.

Great crested newt

72 Toads and frogs propel themselves by kicking back with their hind legs. They use their front legs as a brake for landing when they dive into the water. Large, webbed feet act like flippers, helping them to push through the water.

Frog draws its legs up

Pushes its feet out to the side

The main kick back with toes spread propels the frog forward through the water

Frog closes its toes and draws its legs in and up for the next kick

73

A swimming snake may seem unlikely, but most snakes are experts in the water. Sea snakes can stay submerged for five hours and move rapidly through the depths. European grass snakes are also good swimmers. They have to be because they eat animals that live around water.

I DON'T BELIEVE IT!

Floating sea snakes often find themselves surrounded by fish who gather at the snake's tail to avoid being eaten. When the snake fancies a snack, it swims backwards, fooling the unlucky fish into thinking its head is its tail!

Yellow–bellied sea snake

Banded sea snakes

Paddle–like end to the tail

The bands act like camouflage to help break up the outline of the snake's body.

74

Sea turtles have light, flat shells so they can move along more easily under water. Some have managed speeds of 29 kilometres per hour. Their flipper-like front legs 'fly' through the water. Their back legs form mini-rudders for steering.

▲ The Pacific ridley turtle lives in warm waters all around the world. It feeds on shrimp, jellyfish, crabs, sea–snails and fish.

Nature's tanks

75 Tortoises and turtles are like armoured tanks – slow but very well–protected by their shells. Tortoises live on land and eat mainly plants. Some turtles are flesh-eaters that live in the salty sea. Other turtles, some of which are called terrapins, live in freshwater lakes and rivers.

76 When danger threatens, tortoises can quickly retreat into their mobile homes. They simply draw their head, tail and legs into their shell.

77 Tortoises and turtles are ancient members of the reptile world. They are the oldest living reptiles, and might have been around with the very first dinosaurs, about 200 million years ago. They also live longer than almost any other animal – some for up to 150 years!

▶ The matamata turtle lives only in South America. It is one of the strangest of all turtles, as its head is almost flat, and is shaped like a triangle. It lies on the bottom of rivers and eats fish that swim past.

▶ The Indian softshell turtle is also called the narrow-headed turtle because of its long, thin head. It is a very fast swimmer

◀ The leopard tortoise lives in Africa. It was named after the yellow and black leopard-style markings of its shell.

▶ The hawksbill turtle lives in warm seas all around the world. Its beautiful shell means that it has been hunted so much that it has nearly died out. It is now protected in many countries.

78 Some sea turtles are among nature's greatest travellers. The green turtle migrates an amazing 2000 kilometres from its feeding grounds off the coast of Brazil to breeding sites such as Ascension Island, in the South Atlantic.

Green turtle

ATLANTIC OCEAN

AFRICA

Brazil

Ascension Island

SOUTH AMERICA

Dangerous enemies

79 Animals such as crocodiles, some snakes and snapping turtles make nasty enemies. Snakes are famed for poisoning or strangling prey before gobbling it down. Other reptiles have also found ways of making themselves especially dangerous.

▲ This rat snake has caught its prey, a small meadow vole. It then loops its body around the vole, and stops it breathing by holding it very tight.

▼ The alligator snapping turtle lives in deep rivers and lakes in the USA. To hunt, it opens its mouth so fish can see what looks like a worm, but is actually just bait. When fish come to investigate, the turtle snaps them up!

Bait

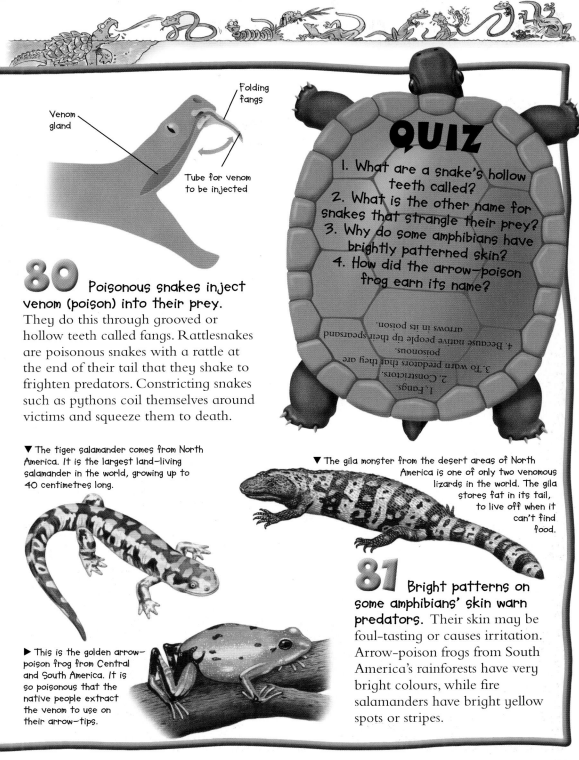

Venom gland

Folding fangs

Tube for venom to be injected

80 Poisonous snakes inject venom (poison) into their prey.

They do this through grooved or hollow teeth called fangs. Rattlesnakes are poisonous snakes with a rattle at the end of their tail that they shake to frighten predators. Constricting snakes such as pythons coil themselves around victims and squeeze them to death.

▼ The tiger salamander comes from North America. It is the largest land-living salamander in the world, growing up to 40 centimetres long.

▼ The gila monster from the desert areas of North America is one of only two venomous lizards in the world. The gila stores fat in its tail, to live off when it can't find food.

▶ This is the golden arrow-poison frog from Central and South America. It is so poisonous that the native people extract the venom to use on their arrow-tips.

81 Bright patterns on some amphibians' skin warn predators.

Their skin may be foul-tasting or causes irritation. Arrow-poison frogs from South America's rainforests have very bright colours, while fire salamanders have bright yellow spots or stripes.

39

Clever mimics

82 From crocodiles and tortoises to lizards and frogs, reptiles and amphibians are masters of disguise. Some blend into their surroundings naturally, while others can change their appearance – perfect for avoiding predators or sneaking up on prey.

Green tree frog

Arum lily frog

Malaysian horned frog

Natal ghost frog

African clawed toad

83 Frogs and toads are experts in the art of camouflage (blending with surroundings). Many are coloured shades of green or green-brown, to look just like leaves, grass or tree bark.

84 Many lizards have green or brown camouflage colouring, too. The chameleon lizard can also change its colour. If it meets an enemy whilst it is walking along a branch, it can stay very still, crouch down and make itself look like the leaves and bark.

87 **The fire-bellied toad has a bright red tummy!** It uses it to distract its enemies. When it's threatened it leaps away to safety, and the quick flash of bright red confuses the attacker, and gives the frog an extra fraction of a second to escape.

◄ This European grass snake is pretending to be dead. It rolls over onto its back, wiggles as if dying, and then lies still with its mouth open and its tongue hanging out!

85 **Some snakes can even pretend to be dead.** They lie coiled up with their tongue hanging out, so that predators will look elsewhere for a meal.

86 **The alligator snapper looks like a rough rock as it lies on the ocean floor.** This cunning turtle has an extra trick up its sleeve. The tip of its tongue looks like a juicy worm, which it waves at passing prey to lure them into its jaws.

ANIMAL DISGUISE!

Make a mask of your favourite reptile or amphibian from a piece of card or a paper plate. Attach some string or elastic to hold it to your head, cut some eye-holes and then colour it all in. You could also try making felt finger puppets – and have a whole handful of reptiles!

Escape artists

88 Reptiles and amphibians form food for other animals. They have developed clever ways to escape predators and survive – at least long enough to grow up and breed.

89 Some salamanders and lizards have detachable tails. If a predator grabs a five-lined tree skink lizard by the tail, it will be left just holding a twitching blue tail! The tail does grow back.

90 The chuckwalla lizard gets itself into tight corners. It can jam itself into a rock crevice, then puff its body up so that predators cannot pull it out.

91

A young blue–tongued skink uses colour as a delay tactic. The lizard simply flashes its bright blue tongue and mouth lining at enemies. The startled predator lets its prey slip away.

92

The Australian shingleback lizard has a tail shaped like a head. By the time a confused predator has worked this one out, the lizard has made its getaway.

▲ The shingleback lizard, which end is its head?

93

Crocodiles can walk on their tails! If they are being threatened they can move so fast they almost leap out of the water! This is called 'tail-walking'.

Close relatives

94 **An alligator isn't quite the same as a crocodile and a frog isn't quite the same as a toad.** These pairs of animals are very similar, but they do have certain differences. If you look carefully, you will be able to spot the small differences between them.

▼ This Nile crocodile lives in Africa. It eats large mammals and birds which it catches from the water's edge while they drink.

Tooth showing

Pointed snout

95 **Alligators are generally smaller than their relations the crocodiles.** They have more rounded snouts and are only found in China and America. Crocodiles are larger, with pointed snouts. They also have two large teeth showing when their mouth is shut.

Shorter, more rounded snout

▼ Caimans are part of the same family as crocodiles and alligators, but are more closely related to alligators. The spectacled caiman gets its name from the ridge between its eyes. This looks like the bridge of a pair of spectacles!

▲ This American alligator lives in the the southeastern United States. It reaches up to 5.5 metres long.

96

Crocodiles and alligators also have some other, very special and rather surprising close relations. They are the closest living relatives of the dinosaurs! The dinosaurs were also reptiles that lived millions of years ago. No one knows why, but all of the dinosaurs died out about 65 million years ago. For some reason, certain other animals that were also around at this time, like crocodiles, alligators and also turtles, survived.

I DON'T BELIEVE IT!

Whether a baby alligator is a girl or boy depends on temperature. A boy will develop in a warm egg, but a girl will develop in a cold one. For crocodiles, it's the other way around!

Short skull

Long legs will become shorter as Protosuchus evolves.

▼ Protosuchus is one of the ancestors of the crocodiles. It lived about 225 million years ago during the Triassic Period. It had quite a short skull, which shows that it had not yet adapted fully for eating fish. It probably ate small lizards.

97

Most frogs live in damp places. Their bodies suit this environment. They tend to have strongly webbed feet, long back legs and smooth skin.

Tree frog

98

Most toads spend their time on dry land. They don't have strongly webbed feet and their skin is warty and quite dry. Toads are normally shorter and squatter than frogs, with shorter legs.

Giant toad

Scary monsters

99 Early explorers told amazing tales of dragons living in faraway lands that few people had visited. It may be that these explorers had somehow seen flying lizards or giant monitor lizards such as the Komodo dragon. Perhaps this is how myths about dragons started.

Komodo dragon

Gould's monitor lizard

Flying dragon

Nile monitor lizard

QUIZ

1. What is usually larger, a crocodile or an alligator?
2. Alligators have two large teeth showing when their mouth is shut. True or false?
3. What is the largest monitor lizard alive today?

1. Crocodiles are usually larger.
2. False, crocodiles have their teeth showing. 3. The Komodo dragon

100 Monitor lizards are long-necked reptiles from Australia, Asia and Africa. The rare Komodo dragon is a monitor from a group of islands in Indonesia, southeast Asia. It is the largest, fiercest lizard alive, up to 4 metres long, weighing 140 kilograms and eating small deer and wild boar.

Index